MW00479435

Building Your
Marriage On
The Rock

A look at marriage through the
lens of God's word

By Pastor Dan Rossborough

Complementary Copy
If you have a need for this
book or know someone that
does. Please feel free to
Take it with you

DEDICATION

To my dad, whom I lost last year—a real man's man. He devoted his life to his family and showed me what it meant to be a man and a father. And to my mother, who has always been there for her children, doing the things that many times went un-noticed but truly made our house a home. Together, they demonstrated the commitment and dedication marriage requires and made sure we all knew we were loved.

CONTENTS

ACKNOWLEDGMENTS

First I would like to say that I wrote this book because I felt compelled to do so by the Spirit and it would be arrogant of me not to mention the Lord Jesus and His vast influence on my life.

And to Pastor George V. Davis, Jr. I offer my undying thanks for his years of biblical teaching that have helped to shape my faith without which none of this would be possible.

1 IN THE BEGINNING

I really am going to start at the beginning, as it is necessary for you to understand the basis that I will be building on. I encourage you to bear with me for just a bit, because unless you understand the foundation of what makes a good marriage, it will be very easy to take things out of context. In the next few chapters, I would like to identify the building blocks that I believe a good marriage should be built on.

In the beginning was God! He is Omnipresent (everywhere), He is Omnipotent (all powerful), He is Omniscient (all knowing). This means that before He said "Let there be light," He knew what He was going to do. He knew Adam and Eve would fall. He knew who you and I would be. He knew, in order to have communion with us, Jesus would have to die on the cross. Yet, He loved us so much He created it all and put us in it. There can be no greater expression of love than that. After God had made Adam and Eve and put them in the garden, He walked with Adam daily. Imagine being able to walk in the garden with God every day. Imagine being able to casually stroll through the garden having a heart-to-heart talk with Him, telling Him your concerns. Imagine being counseled by the creator, who knows the beginning and the end.

After Adam sinned, it created a gulf between he and God. The walks stopped. God could no longer have communion with Adam, or his descendants. It was not possible for sin to coexist with God. God's very nature would destroy it. That is why God would not let Moses see His face, but put him in the cleft of a rock and hid Himself with His hand as He passed by, only allowing Moses to see His back.

> *Exodus 33:20-22 But He said, "You cannot see My face; for no man shall see Me, and live."* *21 And the LORD said, "Here is a place by Me, and you shall stand on the rock. 22 So it shall be, while My glory passes by, that I will put you in the*

cleft of the rock, and will cover you with My hand while I pass by. 23 Then I will take away My hand, and you shall see My back; but My face shall not be seen."

But, Jesus changed all that. We can actually walk daily in the garden with God if we have accepted Jesus as our savior. No longer is it necessary for us to go through rituals and priests to intercede for us. Jesus paid our debts through His death on the cross. It was a free gift to all those that will follow Him. As believers, when God looks on us, He sees us as perfect. Our sin is gone! Washed away by the blood of Christ. Not only can we walk with God daily as Adam did, but God desires us to. We can now stroll through the garden with Him as Adam did—pouring out our concerns and being counseled by the creator, who knows the beginning from the end. It is sad to see all the people who will solicit the services of fortune tellers, who can't truly see the future, when they can have free access to the one that created it all, the one whom truly knows the future.

This brings to mind something God showed me one day in church. I was sitting a few rows behind my pastor's son. He had his arms stretched out on the back of the pew and his four children were nestling in against him—each competing to be the closest. Being a father, it immediately brought back the memories of my children doing the same. At that moment, God spoke to my heart. God desires this from us—to nestle in upon Him. In that moment, I wondered — had I left God desiring my fellowship? Had I left Him waiting? I know even now with all my children grown up, that there is a yearning to see my children and grandchildren. I never feel totally complete until we are all together. If an earthly father can have this desire for his children, how much more does our Heavenly Father desire the same?

Gen 1:26-28 Then God said, "Let Us make man in Our image, according to Our likeness; let them have dominion over the fish of the sea, over the birds of the air, and over the cattle, over all the earth and over every creeping thing that creeps on the earth." 27 So God created man in His own image; in the image of God He created him; male and female He created them. 28 Then God blessed them, and God said to them, "Be fruitful and multiply; fill the earth and subdue it; have dominion over the fish of the sea, over the birds of

*the air, and over every living thing that moves on
the earth."*

He created us in His image and gave us
dominion over all the creatures, but not over each
other. Both male and female were created in His
image. Man is actually the highest of all creation,
because we were made in His image. He created
us to have direct fellowship with Him and desires
to walk with us continually.

Yes, God is with us wherever we go and we
can talk to Him regularly throughout the day, but
it's not the same as having that quiet time of
prayer, reflection, and study. It is in those still
times when we can hear His voice more clearly,
when we have time to contemplate the things that
matter to us—examining our lives and concerns
through the lens of His word. It is only through
that lens that we can judge where we have been
and where we are going, resetting our course
accordingly.

> *Psalms: 1:1-3 Blessed is the man Who walks
> not in the counsel of the ungodly, Nor stands in
> the path of sinners, Nor sits in the seat of the
> scornful; ² But his delight is in the law of the
> LORD, And in His law he meditates day and
> night. He shall be like a tree Planted by the rivers*

of water, That brings forth its fruit in its season,
Whose leaf also shall not wither; And whatever he
does shall prosper.

Before we had such modern inventions like GPS, sailors counted on the stars to navigate the vast oceans. By triangulating their position relative to the stars, they could pinpoint their position accurately. The problem for these early sailors was, if it was a cloudy night and they could not see the stars, they would have to rely on their best guess. They would have to estimate their speed, cross currents, and mass, and make estimates based on their compass heading.

This is known as "dead reckoning." The problem with "dead reckoning" is that it is a guess based on other assumptions. After three or more days, they could be severely off course. If the ocean currents had pushed them off course far enough, they could easily run into an island they could not see, add days to their trip, or miss their destination entirely.

That's the way it is when we neglect spending time with the Lord and His word. The currents of the world can push us off course and lead us into obstacles we don't see, delaying victories or making us miss them completely. God's word is our moral and spiritual GPS. It keeps us on course. It is important that we don't let worldly based relative morality, "generally accepted" science, and similar distractions cloud our judgment and take us off course. If we can't take God at His word, what's the point of believing?

I encourage you to take the time to spend time with God every day. This should not be a chore for us, but something we look forward to. It is a privilege bought with a great price, the blood of Jesus! It is also a way for us to lay our cares at His feet and be refreshed, tuning ourselves to His will. This is a time God looks forward to and we should too.

Gen 2:18-24 The LORD God said, "It is not good for the man to be alone. I will make a helper suitable for him." Now the LORD God had formed out of the ground all the wild animals and all the birds in the sky. He brought them to the man to see what he would name them; and whatever the man called each living creature, that was its name. So the man gave names to all the livestock, the birds in the sky and all the wild animals. But for Adam no suitable helper was found. So the LORD God caused the man to fall into a deep sleep; and while he was sleeping, he took one of the man's ribs and then closed up the place with flesh. Then the LORD God made a

*woman from the rib he had taken out of the man,
and he brought her to the man. The man said,
"This is now bone of my bones and flesh of my
flesh; she shall be called 'woman,' for she was
taken out of man." That is why a man leaves his
father and mother and is united to his wife, and
they become one flesh.*

Adam and all of the creatures on the earth
were made "out of the ground," but none was
suitable as a helper for Adam. Do you think God
was desperately searching for a suitable helper
and didn't know what He was doing? Or could it
be that He knew exactly what He was going to do
and wanted Adam to see that none of the other
creatures was suitable? Maybe He wanted Adam
to value what He had planned for him—Eve.

"Bone of my bone, flesh of my flesh." Eve was
literally made from a part of Adam. Without her,
he was not whole—*"and they become one flesh."* She
was not made from his head so she could rule
over him. She was not made from his foot so he
could tread on her. She was made from his side
so she could come alongside of him as a
helpmeet.

*Gen 3:6-7 When the woman saw that the
fruit of the tree was good for food and pleasing to
the eye, and also desirable for gaining wisdom, she
took some and ate it. She also gave some to her*

husband, who was with her, and he ate it. Then the eyes of both of them were opened, and they realized they were naked; so they sewed fig leaves together and made coverings for themselves.

We all remember the story from Sunday School—it's taught to us early on. But did you ever notice this: "*She also gave to Adam who was with her?*" He was "with" her. So, men, before we go and blame Eve for leading Adam astray, consider Adam's culpability. Is it more than it appears at first glance. Is it possible they had both been eying the fruit for some time?

Most people confronted directly with a choice like this will resist it unless they have already been desiring it or at least considering it. Why is it that the forbidden fruit always looks brighter and more appealing than the rest? Is that truly the case? Is the grass always greener on the other side of the fence? Or is that a perception created by the fact it is forbidden or unobtainable?

What was Adam doing while this conversation with the serpent was going on? He didn't interject, he didn't refute the words of the serpent. We can't really know what Adam was doing, but is it possible he had been eying the fruit as well? Is it possible he was waiting to see what happened with Eve? Would she actually die? What was death? God had told him personally "you must not touch it, or you will die." So how could Adam stand by while she ate the fruit?

We may never know the answer to any of these questions, but was any of this a surprise to God? No, He had a plan! The plan was His grace!

2 GRACE

Understanding grace is paramount to being able to give grace. If we are not able to extend grace in our marriage then we are setting ourselves up for a life of grief.

Grace was God's plan all along. As I said in the previous chapter, God knew Jesus would have to go to the cross before He created us, and Jesus knew it as well. Consider John's words.

John 1:1-5 In the beginning was the Word, and the Word was with God, and the Word was God. He was in the beginning with God. All things were made through Him, and without Him nothing was made that was made. In Him was life, and the life was the light of men. And the light shines in the darkness, and the darkness did not comprehend it.

What John is saying here is that when God spoke things into existence, it was actually Jesus doing the work. That Jesus, knowing full well what would be required of Him, was a willing participant in the creation. In the New Testament, we learn that Jesus is God's word made manifest in the flesh. So if Jesus is God's word and God spoke creation into existence, Jesus, by necessity, actually performed the work of creating.

God's grace is a free gift available to us through the finished work of His son Jesus. It is not something earned. The law is witness to that. And the evidence of this is seen continually throughout the Old Testament. In fact, one of the main purposes of the Old Testament is to teach us this very thing.

The true root of all sin is man wanting to be his own god, doing as he pleases rather than doing what he ought. A man's ego is the primary reason men reject the free gift of salvation—the unwillingness to accept that he is a sinner, is not "good enough," and is unable to earn salvation on his own.

Romans 3:21-26 But now the righteousness of God apart from the law is revealed, being witnessed by the law and the prophets, even the righteousness of God, through faith in Jesus Christ, to all and on all who believe. For there is no difference; for all have sinned and fall short of the glory of God, being justified freely by His grace through the redemption that is in Christ Jesus, whom God set forth as a propitiation by His blood, through faith, to demonstrate His righteousness, because in His forbearance God had passed over the sins that were previously committed, to demonstrate at the present time His righteousness, that He might be just and the justifier of the one who has faith in Jesus.

We can understand this more when we look at the Lord's Prayer. Consider this section: "Forgive us our trespasses." A trespass is willingly doing something we know is a sin. It's one thing to forgive someone for something they did out of ignorance or by accident. It is still another to forgive them for doing it willingly. But Jesus would not have us pray such a thing if God was unwilling to forgive. This is what grace is really about. Grace is not getting what we deserve and receiving God's unmerited favor instead.

However, that is not the end of the prayer. What about this part: "as we forgive those who trespass against us?" I don't know about you, but for me this is easier said than done. That is why Jesus included it in the Lord's Prayer. You see, there must be an act of the will first. We need to decide we are going to forgive, and when unforgiveness rears its ugly head, we have to repent. Yes, I said repent when we fail to forgive someone for intentionally doing something wrong against us. We may not feel like it or want to, but is what the Lord requires of us. It is through this process that God will work out true forgiveness in our hearts.

If the Bible calls us to forgive when anyone trespasses against us, how much more should this apply in our relationship to our spouses? How much more should we strive to forgive them, even when they have done something intentional that has upset us? God said in Isaiah 43:23:

> "I, even I, am He who blots out your transgressions for My own sake; And I will not remember your sins."

And we read in *Hebrews 8:12:*

*"For I will be merciful to their
unrighteousness, and their sins and their lawless
deeds I will remember no more."*

Imagine if we could forgive our spouses to this extent, not remembering their trespasses. We would have nothing to throw in each other's faces during disagreements. But, all of this starts with making a decision to forgive, then trusting the Lord to work the forgiveness in our hearts.

Now, let me elaborate on what it means to make a decision to forgive. It means that every time you feel the urge to remember or dwell on a transgression against you, you instead remember your decision to forgive and seek God's strength in the situation. I don't want to imply it will be easy, but this is part of the struggle we have with the "inner man." While taking a perceived transgression against us to the Lord seems unfair, it is really what we are instructed to do and is beneficial to us in the end.

This brings to memory a situation I faced many years ago within our Senior High Youth Group. Every year we would attend a five-day Christian festival with a lot of speakers and concerts. One particular year, things started to get out of hand. We basically had two factions within the group fighting amongst themselves. I spent the morning praying about how to defuse the situation and the Lord gave me a simple solution. Leave it in His hands!

At lunch I sat them all down and we had a little talk about forgiveness. I reminded them that I had not been present for any of the perceived transgressions and had no way of sorting out the truth. But, God had seen it all. Not only that, but he knew the hearts of all those involved. I explained to them that we were going to take this whole matter to prayer and they were free to bring any grievance they had with each other to the Lord and/or repent for any part they had in it. When we had finished praying, there was a different mood and a new unity within the group. God is able, when we are not.

It is easy to hold a grudge against someone when we perceive a transgression against us. It's another thing to honestly take it to God and make our case. More times than not, we realize very quickly how trivial the transgression actually was. The fastest way to put a grievance in perspective is to take it to the Lord with a full understanding of what He has done for you personally, realizing that God loves the person you have the grievance with just as much as He loves you and that He extends the same grace to them as he extends to you. If you think it doesn't seem fair, just remember how fair it was when God watched His son die on the cross in your place. Trust me, your grievance pales in comparison.

Charles Swindoll once told a story that I will condense for our purposes: The setting was a church member meeting. There was a younger man standing in front. He was airing a grievance and kept repeating the phrase "I just want my rights." After a while, an elderly man stood up in the back of the room and interrupted. "Your rights? You just want your rights?" he exclaimed. "What about your wrongs? Jesus came to take your wrongs."

As believers, we have laid hold of the free gift of salvation Jesus has won for us. But have we fully understood why He did it? It was because of the depth of His love for you that He laid down His life while "we were yet sinners." The deep affection God has for you, that he created you, knowing what Jesus would have to do in order for Him to have communion with you. How valuable you must be to Him. Instead of the misguided, self-esteem the young man in the story was clinging to, what we truly need is a healthy God-esteem, understanding where our value truly lies. This value to Him is where grace begins.

> *Psalm 139:13-16 For You formed my inward parts; You covered me in my mother's womb. I will praise You, for I am fearfully and wonderfully made, Marvelous are Your works, And that my soul knows very well. My frame was not hidden from You, When I was made in secret, And skillfully wrought in the lowest parts of the earth. Your eyes saw my substance, being yet unformed. And in Your book they all were written, The days fashioned for me, When as yet there were none of them.*

I had a real eye-opening experience the first time I watched the movie *Contact* with Jodie Foster. Although the movie storyline is way off-base from reality, the beginning of the movie moved me greatly. The scene opened with Jodie Foster standing on her balcony, staring off into space. The camera was pointed down at her and gradually started to pull back. It went faster and faster as it went higher. She grew smaller in the picture until you couldn't see her anymore, and then it kept going. Eventually, the buildings blended into cities and became spots. The camera kept going and the earth grew smaller until it disappeared. The camera pulled back through the clouds, past the moon, past the planets, through space, past nebulae and other heavenly bodies. At that moment, it hit me—just how big God is and how seemingly insignificant I am.

Yet He knew me, He "formed my inward parts." Thankfully the theater was dark and no one could see the tears streaming down my face. But, as my pastor always said in church, "ain't God good!" When we start to get a glimpse of how great God is and realize how much He cares and desires fellowship with us, we can begin to understand how special His grace is. The more we understand this, the stronger our God-esteem becomes and the more able we are to extend His grace to others and especially to our spouses.

Growing up, I lived in the country. Our small community was surrounded by farmland and woods. My friends and I had a cabin we had built, out in the woods, a few miles from where I lived. We managed to burn it down a few times and subsequently rebuild it. Each time a little bigger and a little better as we got older. The last time we rebuilt it, we were old enough that some of us could drive. As a result, we were able to get better and heavier materials to the construction site.

One of the things we were able to acquire was a large woodstove with a heat exchanger. The town had just built a new barn for their trucks and were discarding it, because it was no longer needed. It was definitely overkill for our little 600-square-foot cabin, but it sure kept us warm and was the source of many memories. In later years I have used this woodstove many times as an example of how God's word and His grace should affect us and how we should share it with others.

The woodstove is heated on the inside by feeding it wood. As the wood burns it heats the stove and heat exchanger. The stove and heat exchanger begin to radiate that heat warming the air and objects around it. The hotter the fire the more heat it produces and the hotter the stove and heat exchanger get. The hotter they get the warmer the air and objects around them become and the further the heat travels.

There are two important factors that determine how large of an area the stove can heat and how quickly it can heat it. How much wood you can put in it and how much surface area it has. The heat exchanger on this particular woodstove had almost as much surface area as the stove itself, making it very efficient at heating the area around it.

As we feed our spirit with God's word it should have an inward effect on us. Heating us from the inside out, so to speak. The more we grow in God's word and come to understand His love for us, and consequently His grace toward us, the more our God-esteem will grow. The more our God-esteem grows the more we will care less about ourselves and more about others. The more we will radiate His love and grace.

The more we can understand how important we are to God and how much He cares for us the easier it is to die to self. And, it becomes much easier to forgive others' trespasses against us. The more we reach out to others the more "surface area we have," the more God will use us to influence others. This is the growth process we should strive for. This is the type of growth that will help marriages stand against the challenges of this world.

3 GOD'S VIEW OF RELATIONSHIPS

One thing the Bible has a plethora of information about is God's view of relationships and some with great promise.

Exodus 20:12 Honor your father and your mother, that your days may be long upon the land which the LORD your God is giving you.

I know this is a book on marriage but it is important that we understand why this is important enough that it comes with a promise.

The family unit is where we begin to learn what it means to be under authority. It is where we learn many of our relationship skills. God intended for mothers and fathers to be earthly examples of His love to their children as they grow and mature. That is why I believe that the deterioration and breakup of families and the family structure in the US is responsible for many of the challenges we face today in our society. Unfortunately, many children are being raised in broken homes, by absentee parents, by abusive parents, or any combination of these. And, even the best parents will still make mistakes. Your childhood may not have been a fairytale and it may be very difficult for you to honor your father or mother. But, none the less it is what God requires.

> *Romans 3:23 …for all have sinned and fall short of the glory of God…*

"All have sinned," this includes your father and your mother. Even if they failed you in one way or another, God still loves them and extends to them the same offer of salvation and grace as He does to you or anyone else. This again may be part of the fight we have with our inner man. The necessity to forgive the trespass of others even if they may have been abusive to us.

That last statement probably raised a few eyebrows so please let me explain. I am not suggesting that you continue to subject yourself to abuse. In fact, if you are in an abusive relationship with anyone, be it a spouse, parent, or anyone else, you need to separate yourself from them. What I am talking about has more to do with attitude and where your heart is.

I think King David is a good example of this. Because of the people's outcry, God appointed Saul as Israel's first king. The Bible tells us God gave them a king that they would have picked. A tall, strong, and handsome man. Saul started out great, giving God the glory for all his victories. But, eventually Saul started to think more highly of himself than he should have. He began to believe that he alone was responsible for the many victories and success of his kingdom. He began taking credit for what God was doing. Because of this and unbeknownst to Saul, God had a plan to replace him with David.

> *1 Samuel 16:11-14 And Samuel said to Jesse, "Are all the young men here?" Then he said, "There remains yet the youngest, and there he is, keeping the sheep."*

> *And Samuel said to Jesse, "Send and bring him. For we will not sit down till he comes here." So he sent and brought him in. Now he was ruddy, with bright eyes, and good-looking. And the LORD said, "Arise, anoint him; for this is the one!" Then Samuel took the horn of oil and anointed him in the midst of his brothers; and the Spirit of the LORD came upon David from that day forward. So Samuel arose and went to Ramah.*

Saul originally embraced David because David had killed Goliath and saved his kingdom. But Saul soon became jealous of David's fame. Because of his enlarged ego Saul decided he would get rid of David. His rage burned against David and he pursued him for years, trying to kill him. However, David determined in his heart to honor Saul. He understood that God had ordained Saul. Even when opportunities arose for David to kill Saul he stayed the hand of his men. In fact, we know that David himself had opportunity to kill Saul twice, yet he spared him.

I'm sure many of David's men found this hard to understand. Saul was pursuing David trying to kill him, so it would be completely understandable for David to want to kill Saul in self-defense. Yet upon learning of Saul's death, David tears his clothes and mourns and weeps for Saul's death. Then he had the young Amalekite put to death for laying a hand on Saul.

> *2 Samuel 1:14-16 So David said to him, "How was it you were not afraid to put forth your hand to destroy the LORD's anointed?" Then David called one of the young men and said, "Go near, and execute him!" And he struck him so that he died. So David said to him, "Your blood is on your own head, for your own mouth has testified against you, saying, 'I have killed the LORD's anointed.'"*

No matter what your mother or father may have done for you or to you, they are still how God brought you into existence. For that you should honor them. For some of us this may be easy, for others it may not be. But that is the command. If you find yourself at odds with your father, mother, or both, it is important that you first forgive them for any offenses, actual or perceived, and learn to honor them. As it was in David's case, it may be necessary to separate yourself from them to protect yourself, but your attitude needs to be in line with God's commands. As I said previously, forgiveness starts as decision followed by determination, trusting God for the rest.

> *1 Peter 2:18-20 Servants, be submissive to your masters with all fear, not only to the good and gentle, but also to the harsh. For this is commendable, if because of conscience toward God one endures grief, suffering wrongfully. For what credit is it if, when you are beaten for your faults, you take it patiently? But when you do good and suffer, if you take it patiently, this is commendable before God.*

What does this have to do with marriage? Nothing and a lot. It is true that this scripture is talking specifically about servants, but it also demonstrates the need for maintaining a Godly attitude in our relationships, some of the purposes for doing so, and helps put our marital relationships in perspective.

Think about it, God is directing servants to be submissive with all fear to their masters, even the harsh ones. And He is not talking about a physical fear, I'm sure He didn't need to tell them that. Rather He is speaking about a spiritual fear. Because it is a credit to them when they endure grief and suffering wrongfully, if they are yielding to the authority of their masters, as onto God. In doing so they become witness of Christ, living out their faith before men.

There is no more powerful witness then living out your faith, honoring and trusting in God, as you endure hardship. It is one thing to praise and honor God in the good times, but people will truly take notice when you do so in difficult situations. So, imagine the witness of a servant honoring and serving a harsh master. Doing for their master as onto the Lord. In the process making their suffering an offering. It may seem unfair, but it is where the Lord has chosen to use them.

Just look at the amazing epistles written by Paul. Many of which were written in dungeons under the most deplorable conditions. They didn't have heat, air conditioning, beds, modern toilets, or cable TV like our modern prisons. They were dark, dreary places. Prisoners had to fight off the rats for their food and the bathroom was a corner of the dungeon. Sickness and disease ran rampant. Yet from this environment Paul penned letters of joy and hope. Paul understood just how temporary our fleshly existence is in the light of eternity and took joy in what he had been saved from and to.

It is arrogant, and ignorant for those of us that claim victory over death through the salvation of Christ, declaring Him Lord, to believe that we deserve better than those that walked before us. That somehow, we should be immune from difficulties and persecution. Instead of asking God "why me?" when difficulty comes our way, we need to understand that unless God allowed it, it could not have happened and that if He allowed it, it has purpose. We may not know the purpose, but we can cling to the fact that there is one and God is in control. I'm not going to wander off into the weeds here because this is a huge subject. But when looking at the relationships between bosses and employees, parents and children, husband and wife, and other relationships where one has authority over another, we have to keep in mind these truths. And, that God is in control!

Matthew 5:38-42 "You have heard that it was said, 'An eye for an eye and a tooth for a tooth.' But I tell you not to resist an evil person.

> *But whoever slaps you on your right cheek, turn the other to him also. If anyone wants to sue you and take away your tunic, let him have your cloak also. And whoever compels you to go one mile, go with him two. Give to him who asks you, and from him who wants to borrow from you do not turn away."*

If you have truly given your life to Christ, whose cheek are they really slapping? Whose cloak are they trying to take? Who are they really compelling to go the mile? If we have given Jesus Lordship over our lives, our lives are His to use as He sees fit. When people come against you to persecute you or harm you, it is actually Jesus they have come against. That is a terrible place for them to be, which is exactly why Jesus told us to pray for our enemies. Because they have put themselves in the position of persecuting Christ. We are called to have mercy on them just as God had mercy on us through Christ. Desiring for them to be saved from their sin and reconciled to Christ as brothers and sisters with us.

So it is in our marriage. If a husband is holding something against his wife and she is a believer, he is at enmity with Christ and so it is with the wife, if she is holding something against her husband and he is a believer, she is at enmity with Christ. The Bible tells us in marriage the "two become one flesh" so whether we are husband or wife holding something against the other not only puts us at enmity with Christ, but also with ourselves.

This brings us back to grace. Just as God shows His grace to us, we are instructed to show grace to our enemies. If we are to show grace to our enemies, how much more so should we be willing to show grace to our husband or wife?

4 PROPER PERSPECTIVE

Ever hear the expression "never judge a man until you have walked a mile in his shoes"? Looking at this under the lens of God's word, I would say this is very sage advice. The point being you have no idea what has happened in another person's life. Their difficulties, their struggles with the inner man, and their life experiences are all part of who they are.

We tend to be quick at justifying our own behavior and to judging others. After all, when it comes to ourselves it is easy to use the excuse, "they don't know what I'm dealing with." We generally have no problem justifying our actions with extenuating circumstances. But that road cuts both ways. We also have no idea what someone else is dealing with. It is necessary for us to come to grips with the fact that "all have sinned and fall short of the glory of God," and that includes you! And that includes me! I cannot count the times I have heard someone say, "how can so and so call themselves a Christian when they do such and such." This attitude is a flat out failure to understand what God has saved us from personally and fully understanding the depths of God's grace. It is very possible that person being judged is fighting battles we know nothing about and may have made great strides and already won great battles in their walk with the Lord. Since we haven't "walked a mile in their shoes," it is impossible for us to know or judge.

I took a course on supervision many years ago and they made a point that I have applied throughout my life and I think it applies here as well. I have no idea if you play golf or not, but for the sake of this point, let's say you haven't. You wake up one morning and decide hey, I'm going to learn to play golf. You get up and go down to the golf course with no idea what to expect, you know nothing about the sport. Eventually, you find your way into the pro shop and their resident instructor just happens to be there and has time to give you a lesson.

After renting some clubs and buying a bucket of balls you head down to the driving range with the instructor. He shows you how to put the ball on the tee and the correct way to swing. He hands you the club and tells you to take a swing. At this point he determines that on your next swing he is going to correct every mistake you made. He is going to make you an expert golfer in that next swing! He spends about fifteen minutes telling you everything you did wrong. You take your next swing and the instructor is beside himself, he can't understand why you didn't do everything exactly as he had told you.

It would likely be a very frustrating experience and there is a good chance it would scare you away from ever trying to play golf again. But I've watched many a well-meaning Christian decide they were going to "disciple" a new believer, and then proceed to lay out all the do's and don'ts, overwhelming the ones they are trying to "disciple." It's even worse when the Holy Spirit works in a fellow believer's life over a stumbling block they may have. Then they immediately assume that they need to play Holy Spirit in everyone else's lives over that issue. The truth is the Spirit works in each of our lives, correcting and guiding us as He sees fit. Where we can make a mistake is to assume that because the Spirit shows us something we should avoid or change in our life it must be for everyone else.

The truth is it may not be a stumbling block for that other person. Or, it may be a stumbling block for them as well, but there is something else the Spirit is working on with them that is more critical. Or perhaps God is planning to use them in a different way than you. A golf pro would not try to fix everything you did wrong on the first swing like in the example. He would take the worst part of your swing and begin there, creating building blocks along the way. So it is with the Holy Spirit. He is not going to try to make you perfect all at once. He will work with the most important things while creating building blocks along the way. Knowing God's plan for you and preparing you accordingly. We have to allow Him to work in each other's lives as He sees fit.

The truth is none of us will obtain perfection until we see Jesus face to face.

1 Corinthians 15:50-55 Now this I say, brethren, that flesh and blood cannot inherit the kingdom of God; nor does corruption inherit incorruption. Behold, I tell you a mystery: We shall not all sleep, but we shall all be changed, in a moment, in the twinkling of an eye, at the last trumpet. For the trumpet will sound, and the dead will be raised incorruptible, and we shall be changed. For this corruptible must put on incorruption, and this mortal must put on immortality. So when this corruptible has put on incorruption, and this mortal has put on immortality, then shall be brought to pass the saying that is written: "Death is swallowed up in victory."

> *"O Death, where is your sting?*
> *O Hades, where is your victory?"*

In the meantime, we have to rely on His grace and mercy. Understanding that we are all sinners as we lift one another up in prayer and encourage each other to grow in His Spirit. Believing that God will work in each person's life as He sees fit. We must not judge our husband or wife based on what "we" think, but rather trust in the Holy Spirit and His ability to bring any necessary changes in the correct timing.

This does not mean we do not challenge someone that is openly living in sin. There are certain things the Bible is very clear on and the church cannot afford to abide with those openly living in sin. How this is handled within the marriage is very dependent on the circumstances, which is one of the reasons I am writing this book.

If we keep our focus on our own walk with Jesus, comparing ourselves to Him, we will be continually reminded of our own shortcomings and need for His grace. This constant reminder of our own need for grace will make it much easier to see others as the Lord does and is particularly important in the marriage. The closer we are to someone, the better we know their faults and the easier it is to become judgmental. The best guard against this is to be ever mindful of our own shortcomings and our own need for grace. As Paul said;

> *1 Timothy 1:15 This is a faithful saying and worthy of all acceptance, that Christ Jesus came into the world to save sinners, of whom I am chief.*

The one thing we see throughout Paul's ministry is that he was acutely aware of his own shortcomings. This is how he was able to keep his perspective throughout his ministry. It is just as important for us to keep our perspective, especially when it comes to our husband or wife.

If we fail to keep that perspective, things can get ugly fast. After all, who can hurt us more than the one we love? Through the intimacy of marriage, it becomes very easy to figure out which buttons to push to get a reaction from our spouse. Unfortunately, if we fail to keep our perspective, emotions become weaponized very quickly. If we retaliate against being hurt with hurt, the situation can spiral out of control.

> *Romans 12:17-21 Repay no one evil for evil. Have regard for good things in the sight of all men. If it is possible, as much as depends on you, live peaceably with all men. Beloved, do not avenge yourselves, but rather give place to wrath; for it is written, "Vengeance is Mine, I will repay," says the Lord. Therefore "If your enemy is hungry, feed him; If he is thirsty, give him a drink; For in so doing you will heap coals of fire on his head." Do not be overcome by evil, but overcome evil with good.*

Now I hope you don't consider your husband or wife an enemy, but if this is how we are to treat enemies, shouldn't we treat a husband or wife better? Not wishing to see coals heaped upon their head, but rather see them reconciled with us. Even in this scripture God's desire is not revenge but to see them turn from their ways.

Just as you have to struggle with the inner man, so does your husband or wife. No matter how well you know them, you are not them. You may know about their childhood, some of their experiences before you met, experiences they've had since, but you didn't live them. We never truly know how something will affect us until it happens and even then, the affect it has is shaped by our past experiences. This helps to explain why two different people will be affected differently from the same experience. Because they have had many life experiences that accumulatively affect how they react to the next and since we have not lived each and every one as they have, we really cannot judge them.

> *Matthew 7:1-6 "Judge not, that you be not judged. For with what judgment you judge, you will be judged; and with the measure you use, it will be measured back to you. And why do you look at the speck in your brother's eye, but do not consider the plank in your own eye? Or how can you say to your brother, 'Let me remove the speck from your eye'; and look, a plank is in your own eye? Hypocrite! First remove the plank from your own eye, and then you will see clearly to remove the speck from your brother's eye."*

What Jesus is plainly telling us is that it is hypocritical of us to judge others unless we ourselves have not sinned. Isn't it interesting how many times we find the person being critical of others is actually guilty of doing what they are criticizing others for? Maybe they have justified it to themselves and seeing it in another person brings them conviction over it. Perhaps, they are well aware of their own guilt and are afraid the other person's actions will raise awareness about the issue and their own guilt will be discovered.

To be truthful, I have caught myself acting this way and I think if most people were honest about it, they would admit the same. And I probably have to say for both of these reasons. This goes back to the self-esteem verses God-esteem issue. Wanting to believe that we are an "ok" person. But, if we can get the proper view of ourselves, God's view, we will realize we are better than "ok." We are justified and forgiven and made holy through Christ's willing work at the cross. God paying such a great price just to have communion with each of us. Not because we earned it, but simply because He loves us. This is the same love He has for everyone including your husband or wife.

From this perspective it is much easier to look past the faults of others. Esteeming them as we do ourselves. How could a disagreement between a husband and a wife arise if both esteemed the other as they do themselves, forgiving their trespasses? Desiring to bless them as God has blessed us and understanding that in the process we are blessing ourselves as "two have become one flesh."

> *Philippians 2:21-4 Therefore if there is any consolation in Christ, if any comfort of love, if any fellowship of the Spirit, if any affection and mercy, [2] fulfill my joy by being like-minded, having the same love, being of one accord, of one mind. [3] Let nothing be done through selfish ambition or conceit, but in lowliness of mind let each esteem others better than himself. [4] Let each of you look out not only for his own interests, but also for the interests of others.*

This is a command given to each of us and is doubly true in a husband and wife relationship. To actually esteem others better than yourself. The one thing you don't see here is an "if." How you act is not dependent on the other person. So many times, we like to justify not doing and acting as we should on the other person's failure to do something or act a certain way.

Unfortunately, we don't get this pass. We are responsible to act according to God's commands regardless of how we may have been treated.

> *Romans 5:6-10 For when we were still without strength, in due time Christ died for the ungodly. [7] For scarcely for a righteous man will one die; yet perhaps for a good man someone would even dare to die. [8] But God demonstrates His own love toward us, in that while we were still sinners, Christ died for us. [9] Much more then, having now been justified by His blood, we shall be saved from wrath through Him. [10] For if when we were enemies we were reconciled to God through the death of His Son, much more, having been reconciled, we shall be saved by His life.*

Jesus having died for us while we were yet sinners, has the right to require us to give the same deference to others. As freely as He has given us His love, forgiveness, and grace, we are to give it to others just as freely. We need to have the proper prospective in our lives, of ourselves and our relationship with the Lord. Only then can we begin to have right relations with others, including our husband or wife.

5 FOR HUSBANDS

Wives, skip this chapter. Please be aware that how well your husband does or does not follow what is written here, or more importantly in scripture, has no bearing on what God has asked of you. It in no way changes your obligation in the marriage. There will also be a similar warning to husbands in the beginning of the chapter "For Wives." Everything in this chapter pertinent to wives will be repeated in the chapter for wives. This chapter is simply tailored toward husbands and the one for wives is tailored toward you.

Husbands, always remember to keep your relationship strong with God. Since God has called on you to be the spiritual leader within the household, it is extremely important for you to be in prayer and fellowship with Him. This is not only for learning and growing, but it also helps to keep you on the right path and should always be the first priority. It is so easy to get distracted from spending time with the Lord, in His word and with fellow believers, as more and more demand is placed on your time. But, keeping on the right track will make life much easier in the long run and goes a long way toward having a strong marriage.

What is God specifically asking husbands to do? Love your wife as Christ loved the church. Think about what it means to love your wife as Christ loved the church.

Eph. 5:25 Husbands, love your wives, just as Christ also loved the church and gave Himself for her…

I could easily write a book just on this subject of how Christ loved the church, but it has already been written. It's called the Bible. Keep in mind that Jesus is part of the trinity, one with the Father. We already discussed the fact that Jesus was with God and a major part of the creation. But, that also means He was present and an active part of the entire Bible story.

Everything in the Bible from the creation through the tribulation was done for the purpose of the church. It was all leading to Jesus on the cross and to the end times when God will finalize His work. Collecting the last few that will be saved. It's all about His love for us, the church, and His desire to have fellowship with us.

A husband that loves his wife properly is much easier to submit to. To love your wife properly you must subdue your selfish desire to serve yourself. You are called to be the head servant.

> *John 13:3-8 Jesus, knowing that the Father had given all things into His hands, and that He had come from God and was going to God, rose from supper and laid aside His garments, took a towel and girded Himself. After that, He poured water into a basin and began to wash the disciples' feet, and to wipe them with the towel with which He was girded. Then He came to Simon Peter. And Peter said to Him, "Lord, are You washing my feet?" Jesus answered and said to him, "What I am doing you do not understand now, but you will know after this." Peter said to Him, "You shall never wash my feet!" Jesus answered him, "If I do not wash you, you have no part with Me."*

What is leadership in the family? Husbands are to give their lives for their wife. Just as in Jesus' example they are to be willing to make themselves a servant. Jesus washed the feet of His disciples, even those of Judas, who Jesus knew was about to betray Him. Husbands are to manage and care for their wife's needs and desires. It makes no difference what your wife may or may not have done. There are no conditions here, it is simply the responsibility of the husband to obey. To love his wife come what may. To be quick to forgive and slow to anger. To put his wife ahead of himself.

Paul taught that men were to rule their own homes well.

> *1 Tim. 3:5 For if a man does not know how to rule his own house, how will he take care of the church of God?*

Not only have you been called to be the loving servant in your home, giving yourself wholeheartedly to this calling. Headship is also the responsibility to lead by action and example as Christ did.

> *John 13:14-17 If I then, your Lord and Teacher, have washed your feet, you also ought to*

wash one another's feet. For I have given you an example, that you should do as I have done to you. Most assuredly, I say to you, a servant is not greater than his master; nor is he who is sent greater than he who sent him. If you know these things, blessed are you if you do them.

The only reason we should need for doing this, is that it is right in the eyes of the Lord. However, it is also beneficial to us. Contrary to what many people believe, God does not just give arbitrary commands. Rather there is reason behind them. Sometimes that reason will be obvious, sometimes not.

Look at the example of Moses. The first time the Israelites complained in the desert about not having water and being thirsty, God instructed Moses to go forward and strike the rock and water poured out of it. The second time this happened, God told Moses to go forward and speak to the rock. But, Moses being angry with the people went to the rock and struck it twice.

Numbers 20:10-12 And Moses and Aaron gathered the assembly together before the rock; and he said to them, "Hear now, you rebels! Must we bring water for you out of this rock?" 11 Then Moses lifted his hand and struck the rock twice

*with his rod; and water came out abundantly, and
the congregation and their animals drank.*

*12 Then the LORD spoke to Moses and
Aaron, "Because you did not believe Me, to
hallow Me in the eyes of the children of Israel,
therefore you shall not bring this assembly into the
land which I have given them."*

Moses had misrepresented God, giving the
appearance that God was angry with the people.
Moses also didn't know that God was using the
situation as an example of His plan for salvation.
The rock represented Christ, who was stricken on
the cross. The water represented forgiveness and
life-giving grace. Striking the rock a second time
gave the impression that it would be necessary for
Christ to be stricken each time forgiveness and
grace were needed. This of course is not true,
Jesus was the perfect sacrifice. His crucifixion and
resurrection were enough. As a result of
misrepresenting God, Moses was not allowed to
enter the promised land.

Not allowing Moses to go into the promised
land may seem extreme to some people, but keep
in mind we see Moses again at the
Transfiguration, he did not lose his salvation.
God was making a point to his people, to obey

and not misrepresent Him. Even when we don't "feel like it" as was true in Moses' case. This goes for us as well. We should not treat our wife harshly but instead show God's love, no matter how "we feel" or what she has done.

The husband and wife relationship in the family is meant to be an example of Christ's relationship to the Father and our relationship to Christ. The wife equal to the husband as Christ is to the Father willfully giving authority to the husband as Jesus did to the Father. The children under the authority of both as we are.

> *Eph. 5:25-27 Husbands, love your wives, just as Christ also loved the church and gave Himself for her, that He might sanctify and cleanse her with the washing of water by the word, that He might present her to Himself a glorious church, not having spot or wrinkle or any such thing, but that she should be holy and without blemish.*

Jesus gave spiritual leadership and counsel to his disciples. Likewise, a husband must take spiritual leadership in the home. Practically, this means you are responsible to be an example in your own spiritual life. Provide for, nourish, and cherish your wife as your own flesh. A one-flesh relationship requires this. In order for you to be able to take care of your own body you must take care of and be sensitive to your wife's needs and desires. To be insensitive to or unwilling to meet her needs is to deny her the love and care you show yourself.

A husband that forces his will on his wife is acting like a dictator. Jesus never forced His will on His disciples or on you. Love never forces its own way.

> *1 Cor. 13:4-7 Love suffers long and is kind; love does not envy; love does not parade itself, is not puffed up; does not behave rudely, does not seek its own, is not provoked, thinks no evil; does not rejoice in iniquity, but rejoices in the truth; bears all things, believes all things, hopes all things, endures all things.*

> *James 3:17 But the wisdom that is from above is first pure, then peaceable, gentle, willing to yield, full of mercy and good fruits, without partiality and without hypocrisy.*

A husband needs to take the feelings and desires of his wife into account when making decisions. In fact, he should put them first. In order to do this, he needs to be willing to consult with her and listen to what she has to say. A husband following God's plan will not try to "control" his wife, dictating what she should wear, who her friends should be, or about anything else. He should allow her the freedom to grow while encouraging her in the word. He takes responsibility to initiate and lead the relationship in a Godly manner. Sometimes doing what is right for your wife may be unpleasant for you. Do you think going through what Jesus did, being beaten, dying on the cross, and taking our sin onto Himself was pleasant for Him?

> *Luke 22:41-44 And He was withdrawn from them about a stone's throw, and He knelt down and prayed, saying, "Father, if it is Your will, take this cup away from Me; nevertheless not My will, but Yours, be done." Then an angel appeared to Him from heaven, strengthening Him. And being in agony, He prayed more earnestly. Then His sweat became like great drops of blood falling down to the ground.*

This is the depth to which Jesus was prepared to go, and went to for the church. Understanding what was before Him. Longing for another way. But, going through with it regardless of the cost to Himself. All while we were yet sinners. When everyone had turned their backs on Him. This puts real meaning to the verse, "*Husbands, love your wives, just as Christ also loved the church and gave Himself for her,*" doesn't it! Husbands, this is where the rubber meets the road. How are you doing? If you are failing at this repent "NOW." Fall on His mercy and ask God to show you how.

It is important that a husband spend time with God often. Both in prayer and in His word. Without that Godly GPS it is very easy for you to start putting your own needs and desires ahead of your wife's. For God to truly be in control you have to spend time with Him, otherwise you will eventually drift off course, causing unnecessary harm to your wife and yourself.

There is real danger in the tendency we have to forget our need for God during the times of plenty. When things just seem to be going great. It's never intentional. Usually we don't even realize we are doing it. This is how the enemy works, he tries to get us focused on other things. Trust me, if you fall into this trap you will soon live to regret it.

The Israelites needed to learn this lesson over and over. In fact, it is one of the primary themes of the Old Testament. It seemed every time God brought them victory they would gradually drift away from Him. Taking on more and more of the rituals and customs of the world around them. Eventually they would become apostate. This is why it is important to be in fellowship with other godly believers, encouraging one another in God's word.

Husbands, when you do stumble, and you will, we all do, do not be afraid to seek forgiveness from your wife. Admitting our failures and seeking forgiveness is not a sign of weakness, it is a sign of strength. It is the sign of a mature Christian doing the right thing.

It is also a powerful witness for our families, our churches, and to the world, as Godly men willingly humble themselves. So many times, Christians have the false idea that they have to hide their failures, for fear of being called hypocrites or being seen as failures. It only becomes hypocritical when you attempt to hide it. The only failure is not admitting that we have fallen short.

Yes, we subscribe to a set of biblical values that are what we strive to live up to. However, we also believe in God's grace, confessing we are sinners in need of Jesus' salvation. Failing in our walk and not confessing it and seeking forgiveness is to hide the best part. The best witness we can have is to show the whole story. Then we are not hypocrites, not failures, but victors over sin. Saying what we aspire to, admitting we don't always win in our battle with the flesh, and demonstrating God's grace and forgiveness when we fail!

Jesus as our head, initiated our entire salvation by humbling Himself and taking the form of a servant.

> *I John 4:17-19 Love has been perfected among*
> *us in this: that we may have boldness in the day of*
> *judgment; because as He is, so are we in this*
> *world. There is no fear in love; but perfect love*
> *casts out fear, because fear involves torment. But*
> *he who fears has not been made perfect in love. We*
> *love Him because He first loved us.*

In short, a husband needs to have a good relationship with the Lord and cannot do so without being obedient to His will. The precepts God has given in Ephesians about marriage are not optional. The responsibility of each partner does not depend on the actions of the other. Both the husband and the wife are responsible to God for how well they follow His precepts regardless of how well their spouse does.

As evidence let me touch on other scriptures that can help shed light on this.

> *Matthew 5:31-32 "Furthermore it has been*
> *said, 'Whoever divorces his wife, let him give her*
> *a certificate of divorce.' But I say to you that*
> *whoever divorces his wife for any reason except*
> *sexual immorality causes her to commit*
> *adultery; and whoever marries a woman who is*
> *divorced commits adultery."*

Gods goal it to strengthen the marriage. There is no but, and, nor or here. Even in the case of sexual immorality, divorce is not required but allowed. In the case of sexual immorality, we are actually encouraged to forgive, but allowed to divorce if we are not able to. Sexual immorality is a huge betrayal and is an issue that cuts to the heart of a marriage. We may be able to overcome it with the help of the Lord, but it requires true repentance on the part of the guilty party.

> *Matthew 5:43-48 "You have heard that it was said, 'You shall love your neighbor and hate your enemy.' But I say to you, love your enemies, bless those who curse you, do good to those who hate you, and pray for those who spitefully use you and persecute you, that you may be sons of your Father in heaven; for He makes His sun rise on the evil and on the good, and sends rain on the just and on the unjust. For if you love those who love you, what reward have you? Do not even the tax collectors do the same? And if you greet your brethren only, what do you do more than others? Do not even the tax collectors do so? Therefore you shall be perfect, just as your Father in heaven is perfect."*

How much more so shall you love your wife? After all, she is the one you chose. You stood before God and promised to love and honor her come what may. It is sad to see divorce running rampant in the church. As if it is somehow acceptable to God. I have even heard other Christians say it's no big deal, sometimes things just don't work out. Well it is a "big deal!" Jesus was very clear about this. If we are able to keep our proper perspective with God and apply His teaching about dealing with others to our marriages, divorce should not even be a possibility. It should not be on our radar. There is no way for you to have obeyed all of Jesus' commands to forgive and yet want to divorce your wife.

If you love her as yourself, as you are directed to do with your neighbor; if you bless her, even if she curses you, and do good to her, as you are commanded to do with an enemy; if you forgiver her trespasses, as you are commanded to do for everyone; how is it possible for you to be at enmity with her? The answer is it is not! None of this depends on her, it is your responsibility. You can't claim to be "good Christians" if you don't have peace with your wife. That does not necessarily mean she is at peace with you. Just that your attitude is in the right place and you are doing what you are supposed to do and are only seeking her good.

You can't control what your wife does, but you can control what you do. How you react in various situations. It is entirely possible that your wife may never yield herself to God's will and possibly even divorce you. God will not violate her free will. In any case, you should be seeking reconciliation and it should break your heart to see her turning her back on what God has called her to do, as it does Him. In reality, if you are honest and do some soul searching you will likely find some issues you need to work on as well.

Mark 12:29-30 Jesus answered him, "The first of all the commandments is: 'Hear, O Israel, the LORD our God, the LORD is one. And you shall love the LORD your God with all your heart, with all your soul, with all your mind, and with all your strength.' This is the first commandment. And the second, like it, is this: 'You shall love your neighbor as yourself.' There is no other commandment greater than these."

"There is no other commandment greater than these." To love the Lord our God with all our hearts we have to love our neighbor as ourselves. Do we not owe the same to the one we have chosen to wed? As Christians, we are all called to believe in Christ and if we have truly given our lives to Him we need to follow his precepts, regardless of what others do. In doing so we will be blessed and are successful as Christians. You see success for a Christian comes down to a simple thing. Did you do what He has told you to do? The results are up to Him, we are only to obey.

In the marriage it is very important that we understand and apply what God has shown us. We have an enemy that seeks to destroy. This is why we have to be careful about the counsel we seek. The only true counsel we should need is God's word, and if we seek out others for support we should be careful to weigh their counsel against the scripture. They should be lifting up both of you and continually pointing you to the scriptures and God's counsel, never taking a side.

This is why it is dangerous to turn to parents and friends as they are prone to take a side. Better a matter can be settled between the wife, husband, and the Lord. Marital discourse can only occur if both the husband and the wife have turned their backs on what God has called them to do.

Be careful of those who seek to delve into past hurts and ill feelings. But look for those that will continually challenge you with this question: "Are you doing what God has called you to do in the marriage?" This is what matters, that we are obedient to Him. This is regardless of where our spouse is at. If you have not been, it is up to you to repent, seek forgiveness, and mend your ways. Just as Jesus put no condition on us for salvation, but showed unimaginable love by forgiving us while we were still at enmity with Him. So, you

MUST forgive your wife and do what He has called us to do.

6 FOR WIVES

Husbands, skip this chapter. Please be aware that how well your wife does or does not follow what is written here, or more importantly in scripture, has no bearing on what God has asked of you. It in no way changes your obligation in the marriage. There is also a similar warning to wives in the beginning of the chapter "For Husbands." Everything in this chapter pertinent to husbands was also included in the chapter for husbands. This chapter is simply tailored toward wives and the one for husbands is tailored toward you.

Always remember to keep your relationship strong with God, this is always the first priority. It will be difficult for you to be the wife God has called you to be, if you neglect spending time with Him in prayer and in His word. This should be the foundation of every marriage. This is not only for learning and growing, but it also helps to keep you on the right path and should always be the first priority. It is so easy to get distracted from spending time with the Lord, in His word and with fellow believers, as more and more demand is placed on your time. But, keeping on the right track will make life much easier in the long run and goes a long way toward having a strong marriage.

What is God specifically asking wives to do? Submit to your husbands.

> *Eph. 5:22-24 Wives, submit to your own husbands, as to the Lord. For the husband is head of the wife, as also Christ is head of the church; and He is the Savior of the body. Therefore, just as the church is subject to Christ, so let the wives be to their own husbands in everything.*

Submission of the wife to the husband brings order to the family. As our bodies can only function with one head, so the family can only have one head. This is true in any business or organization. It is even true in the Trinity as Jesus and the Holy Spirit are coequal to the Father yet place themselves under His authority. So, it should be with the wife, being equal with the husband, yet willingly placing herself under the authority of the husband.

To some women this may seem unfair or chauvinistic. But, it is what the Lord commands of you. Not to "keep you down" or make you a "slave," but to free you. Freedom comes through Christ's work on the cross. Through His work we were set free from sin. If we truly realize what it is He has done for us, then we should willingly submit to His Lordship, giving our lives freely to Him. If we have truly given our lives to Him, they are His to do as He sees fit. We should be able to willingly and wholeheartedly follow His commands. Understanding that in doing so we are honoring Him. This is where true freedom comes from. Dying to self and following Him.

I have heard women in church say things like, "They may be the heads of the family, but we can turn their heads." Is this really submitting as on to the Lord? Why would you want to turn your husband's head? Wouldn't it be better for him to be following the Lord and for the Lord to be guiding his steps? The true root of sin is man desiring to do his own will, what he wants instead of obeying the Lord. Is that not what these types of attitudes are about? Getting your way.

Romans 8:28 And we know that all things work together for good to those who love God, to those who are the called according to His purpose.

Even if your husband is not as "spiritual" as you think he should be, your faith needs to be in the Lord. Even if your husband is the Godliest man around, he will make mistakes. In either case or anywhere in between, remember God is in control and will work everything for your good if you love him. Even when your husband makes a mistake!

The husband and wife relationship in the family is meant to be an example of Christ's relationship to the Father and our relationship to Christ. The wife equal to the husband as Christ is to the Father willfully giving authority to the husband as Jesus did to the Father. The children under the authority of both as we are.

This willful submission to your husband is an example to your children. When they see this submission it helps them to understand how to submit in the family and to God.

Submission does not mean you become a slave and can't have opinions or make choices for yourself. Submission does not mean that you are inferior to your husband. Scriptures everywhere affirm a woman's equality to her husband, and a woman to a man.

Gal. 3:26-29 For you are all sons of God through faith in Christ Jesus. For as many of you as were baptized into Christ have put on Christ. There is neither Jew nor Greek, there is neither slave nor free, there is neither male nor female; for you are all one in Christ Jesus. And if you are Christ's, then you are Abraham's seed, and heirs according to the promise.

It does mean that you need to yield to your husband's decisions, as he is the head and ultimately responsible to the Lord for the spiritual wellbeing of your family. There are limitations to your submission. Specifically, if you are asked to do something that violates scripture or your conscience before God. You must obey God rather than man.

Acts 5:26-29 Then the captain went with the officers and brought them without violence, for they feared the people, lest they should be stoned. And when they had brought them, they set them before

the council. And the high priest asked them,
saying, "Did we not strictly command you not to
teach in this name? And look, you have filled
Jerusalem with your doctrine, and intend to bring
this Man's blood on us!"

But Peter and the other apostles answered and
said: "We ought to obey God rather than men."

Submission is an attitude of love, respect, and gentleness. Submission means the wife willingly accepts the authority that God has given her husband over the family. True submission requires the wife to resist the temptation to manipulate her husband into doing her will, and instead lift him up in prayer that he may find God's will. Submit to God by submitting to your husband. The only way to truly submit to God is through obedience to Him.

In short, a wife needs to have a good relationship with the Lord and cannot do so without being obedient to His will. The precepts God has given in Ephesians about marriage are not optional. The responsibility of each partner does not depend on the actions of the other. Both the husband and the wife are responsible to God for how well they follow His precepts regardless of how well their spouse does.

As evidence, let me touch on other scriptures that can help shed light on this.

> *Matthew 5:31-32 "Furthermore it has been said, 'Whoever divorces his wife, let him give her a certificate of divorce.' But I say to you that whoever divorces his wife for any reason except sexual immorality causes her to commit adultery; and whoever marries a woman who is divorced commits adultery."*

Gods goal it to strengthen the marriage. There is no but, and, nor or here. Even in the case of sexual immorality, divorce is not required but allowed. In the case of sexual immorality we are actually encouraged to forgive, but allowed to divorce if we are not able to. Sexual immorality is a huge betrayal and is an issue that cuts to the heart of a marriage. We may be able to overcome it with the help of the Lord, but it requires true repentance on the part of the guilty party.

> *Matthew 5:43-48 "You have heard that it was said, 'You shall love your neighbor and hate your enemy.' But I say to you, love your enemies, bless those who curse you, do good to those who hate you, and pray for those who spitefully use you and persecute you, that you may be sons of your Father in heaven; for He makes His sun rise on the evil and on the good, and sends rain on the just and on the unjust. For if you love those who love you, what reward have you? Do*

not even the tax collectors do the same? And if you greet your brethren only, what do you do more than others? Do not even the tax collectors do so? Therefore you shall be perfect, just as your Father in heaven is perfect."

How much more so shall you love your husband? After all, he is the one you chose. You stood before God and promised to love and honor him come what may. It is sad to see divorce running rampant in the church. As if it is somehow acceptable to God. I have even heard other Christians say it's no big deal, sometimes things just don't work out. Well it is a "big deal!" Jesus was very clear about this. If we are able to keep our proper perspective with God and apply His teaching about dealing with others to our marriages, divorce should not even be a possibility. It should not be on our radar. There is no way for you to have obeyed all of Jesus' commands to forgive and yet want to divorce your husband.

If you love him as yourself, as you are directed to do with your neighbor; if you bless him, even if he curses you, and do good to him, as you are commanded to do with an enemy; if you forgive his trespasses, as we are commanded to do for everyone; how is it possible for you to be at enmity with him?

The answer is it is not! None of this depends on him, it is your responsibility. You can't claim to be a "good Christian" if you don't have peace with your husband. That does not necessarily mean he is at peace with you. Just that your attitude is in the right place and you are doing what you are supposed to do and are only seeking good for him.

You cannot control what your husband does. But you can control your own actions. As Christians, we are all called to believe in Christ and if we have truly given our lives to him we need to follow his precepts, regardless of what others do. In doing so we will be blessed and are successful as Christians. You see, success for a Christian comes down to a simple thing. Did you do what He has told you to do? The results are up to Him, we are only to obey.

In the marriage it is very important to understand and apply what God has shown us. We have an enemy that seeks to destroy. This is why we have to be careful about the counsel we seek. The only true counsel we should need is God's word, and if we seek out others for support we should be careful to weigh their counsel against the scripture. They should be lifting up both of you and continually pointing you to the scriptures and God's counsel, never taking a side. This is why it is dangerous to turn to parents and friends as they are prone to take a side.

It is better that a matter can be settled between the wife, husband, and the Lord. Marital discourse can only occur if both the husband and the wife have turned their backs on what God has called them to do. Be careful of those who seek to delve into past hurts and ill feelings. But look for those that will continually challenge you with this question: "Are you doing what God has called you to do in the marriage?" This is what matters, that we are obedient to him. This is regardless of where our husband is at. If you have not been, it is yours to repent and mend your ways. Just as Jesus put no condition on us for salvation but showed unimaginable love by forgiving us while we were still at enmity with Him. So, you MUST forgive your husband and follow the Lord's leading.

7 THE COUNSEL OF OTHERS

I touched on this subject in the chapters for wives and husbands, but I believe this is one of the major factors leading to divorce today that is not often discussed, so in this chapter we will look a lot deeper.

We really need to understand that we do have an enemy that seeks to destroy as much of God's creation as he possibly can.

> *1 Peter 5:8 Be sober, be vigilant; because your adversary the devil walks about like a roaring lion, seeking whom he may devour.*

There is a reason this passage is in the Bible. The threat is real. Some people will take this verse as saying you can lose your salvation. I do not subscribe to that theory and believe there are many other scriptures that refute that belief. My belief is that you cannot lose your salvation if you have truly confessed Christ and turned your life over to Him. But, that Satan will certainly try to silence you and attempt to void your witness. Either way it is a bad situation.

The enemy also knows that the family is an important building block for children. Teaching them to have the proper respect for God and others. Demonstrating to them what it means to be under authority and the proper use of authority. Satan knows that breaking up marriages is a good way to bring disfunction into a family and distort what God has designed. So, it only stands to reason that if you are consulting others about issues within your marriage, the enemy will seek to influence the counsel you are getting, and it may not be as obvious as you would think.

Personally, I find it hard to believe that Adam and Eve were just strolling through the garden one day and the serpent was able to convince them to eat the forbidden fruit so easily. I have a suspicion that they had been eyeing the fruit for some time. Also, the Bible really does not give us a time frame on Eve's conversation with the serpent. This could have easily happened over days.

Let's be honest, we have all committed transgressions. It is seldom just a quick thing that we do. It usually starts with a thought that grows over time until we can somehow justify it to ourselves. This is how the enemy works, because he knows it is effective. He is not going to make it obvious.

Getting counsel from strangers or acquaintances. It probably seems silly that I would suggest you might seek advice from someone you don't really know, but it's not as farfetched as it may sound. It happens all the time and usually without intending to.

For example, say one day you find yourself working with a group of people at work, church, or for any other organization. As usually happens there will be a lot of small talk and maybe a few people that know each other engaged in a deeper conversation. Eventually you start to feel comfortable with one or two people and join in conversation. Nothing too deep, just general stuff. As typically happens, as people in the group get to know more about each other, the subjects get deeper. Eventually someone brings their relationship in to the conversation. Before you know it, you are sharing about yours.

The problem is you really don't know them very well and they only know what you have told them about your husband or wife. So, how good could their counsel be? But worst of all, having your grievances acknowledged even by a stranger gives them credibility in your own mind. Making it hard to be objective about the truth and even harder to forgive if we have been wronged. But forgive is what we are supposed to do.

At best, you have built a relationship with someone based on sharing each other's personal problems and are getting advice that is suspect. But, what if that person sees you solving your personal problems as a threat to your friendship, because you will not "need" them anymore? How good will the advice be then? Or worst case, that it leads to an affair, as happens all too often when that confidant is someone from the opposite sex. Many times, leading to the destruction of two families in the process! Keep in mind that, that sympathetic ear does not live with you. It is easy to be sympathetic from a distance. Especially when hearing only one side.

Be careful about sharing about your relationship casually or being drawn into these types of personal conversations. The enemy is at large seeking those he may devour. He will use any means available to him. Don't open this doorway to him.

Seeking counsel of friends and family.
These are the people that should love you, know you well, and only want the best for you. That is probably all true. What is also true, is that although they may know your husband or wife better than an acquaintance, how well do they really know them? And, how much of what they know about them is through the filter of your eyes?

Honestly, how objective do you think they can really be? First, they are your friends or family and should be predisposed to take "your" side. Would you expect less? Then, they are only hearing "your" side about someone they don't truly know. What they do know about your husband or wife is through the filter of your eyes or at least influenced by their feeling for you. How objective do you think this advice will be? No matter how much they love you or how well intentioned, it is unlikely the advice will be truly objective. Is this something you want to rely on?

Seeking professional counsel. This can be very dangerous, because these are people that have "gone to school for it" and been "trained" in it, giving them credentials. But, they are still people and they do not all have the same backgrounds or beliefs. Although, they are supposed to be objective, their experiences and beliefs are going to influence how they think, just like it does for anyone else. Some more than others depending on how well they can separate themselves from their past.

I'm not saying they are all bad by any means, but you better get to know a lot more about them before you put credence in what they say. Always examine it against God's word. Truth be told, if they are doing anything except helping you deal with your inability to keep God's commands for you and how you are to conduct yourself in the marriage, they are not doing what is best for you. God knows what he is doing and knows the best way for a marriage to work. His precepts are the best way.

In all of these cases keep in mind, you are dealing with people that have their own problems and views. That have egos, bad experiences, wrong beliefs, and a host of human short comings that will influence their advice to you. On top of that we have an enemy that seeks to destroy, muddying up everything that he can and will prey on any or all of those shortcomings.

Issues within your marriage are best settled between you, your husband or wife, and the Lord. If for some reason you find yourself unable to forgive and do what you are called to do in the marriage, seek out people that will strengthen and encourage you in doing what it is God has called you to do. Reject the counsel of those that do not understand these precepts and weigh everything against God's word.

> *Ephesians 6:10-18 Finally, my brethren, be strong in the Lord and in the power of His might. Put on the whole armor of God, that you may be able to stand against the wiles of the devil. For we do not wrestle against flesh and blood, but against principalities, against powers, against the rulers of the darkness of this age, against spiritual hosts of wickedness in the heavenly places. Therefore take up the whole armor of God, that you may be able*

to withstand in the evil day, and having done all, to stand.

Stand therefore, having girded your waist with truth, having put on the breastplate of righteousness, and having shod your feet with the preparation of the gospel of peace; above all, taking the shield of faith with which you will be able to quench all the fiery darts of the wicked one. And take the helmet of salvation, and the sword of the Spirit, which is the word of God; praying always with all prayer and supplication in the Spirit, being watchful to this end with all perseverance and supplication for all the saints.

8 SEPARATION / DIVORCE / REMARRIAGE

The Bible is quite clear on the subjects of separation and divorce. In fact, it says the only acceptable reason for divorce is sexual immorality. So why is divorce running rampant in the church? Because Christians have selective hearing when it comes to the scriptures, believing only those scriptures that are convenient to them.

Unfortunately, there are a lot of separated or divorced Christians out there and many of those that have divorced have remarried. There will likely be many others that will become separated or divorced when their husband, wife, or themselves disregards God's will. What do we do in these situations?

There is actually good reason for a separation in the Christian marriage, however, the ultimate goal should always be reconciliation. Even though divorce is allowed for sexual immorality, reconciliation is still the preferred outcome. As I discussed previously, it is important that you are sure you are doing as God has called you to do in the marriage.

1 Corinthians 7:10 Now to the married I command, yet not I but the Lord: A wife is not to depart from her husband. [11] But even if she does depart, let her remain unmarried or be reconciled to her husband. And a husband is not to divorce his wife.

If you are in an abusive marriage then I believe you need to separate from your abuser immediately. But be careful, while physical abuse is easily defined, mental abuse is not. It is very easy to claim mental abuse and use it as an excuse. But, God knows the truth, He is not fooled.

This is one of those areas where the counsel of others can really become an issue. As humans we tend to embellish when telling "our side" of an issue. Combining that with the fact that most of the people we like to confide in are predisposed to take "our side" can lead them to having a false understanding of what really happened. This in turn can lead to them giving bad advice, while trying to support us, and will help to cement our embellished accounts as fact in our own minds. God knows the truth so be careful not to let yourself be fooled. Be double sure that your perception of "mental abuse" is genuine. And, be triply sure you are not just using it as a bargaining chip to get your way.

If you are separated for any reason other than sexual morality or abuse you may want to rethink your situation. If the separation was your idea then I would suggest you are not in a right position with God over this. There is no way that you can be following His commands as I outlined previously and still feel compelled to separate from your husband or wife. How can you be at enmity with them if you have forgiven them?

If the separation was not due to sexual immorality or abuse and it was your husband's or wife's idea, I would suggest you try to reason with them about the situation. If they are determined to stay separated there is nothing you can do about that. But, I believe it is clear you are to seek reconciliation.

If you have divorced your husband or wife already for reasons other than sexual immorality or your husband or wife divorces you in disregard to the scriptures, and neither has remarried, the obvious answer is to seek reconciliation.

> *1 Corinthians 7:10-11 Now to the married I command, yet not I but the Lord: A wife is not to depart from her husband. But even if she does depart, let her remain unmarried or be reconciled to her husband. And a husband is not to divorce his wife.*

Based on this scripture, I would say that, if you cannot be reconciled, and your ex has kept from sexual immorality and does not remarry, you need to do the same and remain unmarried, hoping for reconciliation at some point.

If you have done your part and truly sought reconciliation and your wife or husband is having none of it, then you need to repent for your part in the failed marriage. The Lord is able and faithful to forgive. But that is not license to just move forward into another relationship, unless you have the confirmation from the Lord. I suggest you take this question to the Lord in prayer.

Let me just say, if you believe the Lord has given you confirmation that it is okay to move forward to pursue another relationship, you need to be very sure of your answer. There is no such thing as a gray area for a believer. If you don't know if something is permissible then it is not. Even if you can't find any scripture that directly forbids it.

This may sound restrictive to you, but let me explain my reasoning. If you are faced with a situation where you don't know if something is permissible or not, why do you have that doubt? If the scriptures do not specifically forbid it, what is the dilemma? Something in your conscience has you concerned about taking this action. Do not forget that when you are a believer the Spirit indwells you. It could very well be the Spirit warning you. Going forward would be denying the Spirit's warning.

And even if it is not a warning from the Spirit and you go ahead, are you not saying to God that you don't know if it is an offense to Him, so you're just going to do it? Is this not indifference to the Lord's desires? Basically saying, your desires are more important than His. Honestly, if this was not something "you wanted" you would not do it. This is the root of all sins, putting your will ahead of God's.

Is it not better to say that you don't know if it is permissible and you will refrain on the chance that it is not, because you love Him enough that you do not want to take the chance? How you handle these types of choices lays bare the truth of where your heart is. And where your heart is, is what really matters.

If you or your ex have already remarried, then repent of your part in the divorce. If you were the one that instigated the divorce or have fault in it, ask forgiveness from your ex, repent, and move on. Trust that the Lord is able to forgive and restore. In either case there is nothing you can do to undo what has been done. Divorcing the new husband or wife to reconcile with the previous would be just as bad as divorcing the first time. You can't undo what has been done!

The point is, God understands we will make mistakes, we will sin, we will transgress. We can't use this for license to just do as we want and then fall on His grace, particularly when it comes to our marriages, but when we do fall, His grace is sufficient for us. When we fall it is important that we confess what we have done and that we look to God for guidance on how to move forward.

Now, regardless of how you got here, if you have remarried or get remarried there are some pitfalls you need to look out for. The first of which is that one or both of you has already been in a marriage. This can lead to comparisons being made, comparing your new husband or wife to the previous, and them doing the same with you.

This can become a source of contention when the new husband or wife does not do something the same way as the previous one, good or bad. You can easily ascribe an innocent act done by your new husband or wife as the same bad habit of your ex, assuming they are going to act the same, when it may not be true. A good example of this would be if you divorced your first husband or wife because they committed adultery. An innocent act by your new husband or wife could be similar enough to something your ex had done that it invokes fear that your new husband or wife is about to have an affair or already has, leading to mistrust when there is no reason for it.

I could go on and on about situations like this. It could have to do with how to discipline children, taking out the trash, you name it. It is very easy to jump to conclusions about someone's motives, especially if you perceive you have been burned before in that manner. But, all of the precepts we have discussed from the previous chapters apply and you need to be doubly on guard against attacks from the enemy in your new marriage. He will try to use previous failures on either of your parts against both of you.

If you have children from a previous marriage, regardless of their age, it is very important that you make it okay for them to love their other parent. Children are usually the ones that suffer the most as a result of divorce. The last thing they need is to be in a tug-of-war between their parents. No matter how your ex is behaving, it is not your children's fault, do not put them in the middle of it.

> *Luke 6:35 But love your enemies, do good, and lend, hoping for nothing in return; and your reward will be great, and you will be sons of the Most High. For He is kind to the unthankful and evil.*

Just because it is your ex, these commands do not go away. You cannot dictate how your ex acts, but you can control how you do! And for the sake of your children, I hope you do!

It is also important for you to be aware that they will need to make adjustments and may be resistant to allow a new person into the family. This can be quite a balancing act when remarrying. You have to make sure they do not feel like you are trying to replace them in your life or that you are trying to have your new husband or wife replace their other parent. All this while keeping your feelings for them from interfering with your relationship with your new spouse.

What if you have remarried and have stepchildren? I met a man once in a men's Bible study who had remarried and had a thirteen-year-old stepson. He spent a good fifteen to twenty minutes complaining about how bad his stepson was. In fact, you would have thought he was the devil. You could see the hatred this man had for this little boy. When he finally wound down I looked at him and said, "You can't love your wife properly, if you don't learn to love her child." He went ballistic!

He could not believe that I would suggest he didn't love his wife. He loved her so much and I had no right to suggest otherwise. But, that's not what I said, I said, "love her properly." We can "love" for many different reasons, but children are a part of their parents, how can you properly love one without the other? I know the Bible says the wife is to obey the husband, but the husband is to love his wife as Christ loves the church. I can't imagine Christ would reject this thirteen-year-old child that has suffered through the trauma of his parents' divorce. I also don't know how you can love your wife as Christ loves the church and try to pit her against her child. How could you put her through such a thing? This was selfishness on his part.

We just read in Luke 6:35 that we are to love our enemies. What this man refused to accept was that he needed to love this little boy that he saw as an enemy. I tried to explain to him that you can love someone even when you are not happy with them. He was having none of it. It is really sad to see something like this happen. I only met the man this one time, as I was just visiting the Bible study that day, but I suspect that if this man did not change his ways, he is either divorced again or in a very contentious marriage.

If you are remarried and the person you married has children, you need to heed this well. Nowhere did Jesus say it is okay to hate a little child. In fact, we are warned against even hindering them.

It only stands to reason that all of the scriptures we have read so far about loving one another, loving neighbors, loving enemies applies to your stepchildren. But I would go even further. I would say to love your new husband or wife properly, you need to learn to love their children as your own. This is also the best way to have harmony in the home.

Now, I am not naive enough to think you will love them like your own the moment you meet them, and you probably will not by the time you say "I do." But, this is a decision you should make and frankly a promise you should make to your betrothed. It will take work, a lot of prayer and soul searching to make it happen, and will pay dividends when you succeed.

Maybe you lived through a divorce as a child and have some understanding of what it is like. If not, you need to think about how it must feel for your stepchildren to have gone through this. How confusing the whole situation is for them. Do not try to immediately become their buddy. Give them some time and space to work things out. Let them come to you. If they are involved in sports, band, choir, or other activities, be involved. Go to the games, concerts, or other things like that. Make yourself available and build common ground. Start slow and build a relationship. These things take time. They need to learn they can trust you.

When they do things that upset you, and they will, try to imagine how you would react if it was your own child, and react in kind. If you don't have children, imagine how Jesus would react. It is important you keep yourself in check, not overreacting. You can love someone even when they disappoint you. Love takes time to build. Be willing to forgive and move forward. Your concern should be doing what is best for them. In the process you will eventually build the bonds that let you love them as your own.

Above all do not try to come between them and their biological parent, no matter how that parent is acting. You will lose that one big time. If there is contention between your husband or wife and their ex, do not take sides with the children and encourage your husband or wife to take a biblical approach to the issues. The children need to feel free to love both of their parents, without shame. Most importantly, pray and be in God's word.

It is my hope they this chapter is irrelevant to you and you have not had to deal with the issues addressed in it and that you never will. But to those of you that it is relevant, my hope is that you move forward from here with a right mind and clear conscience. I have covered a lot of situations here and some of what was said is what I believe based on what I have read in God's word. This is not a substitute for you spending time with the Lord, working out your answers. I believe what I have said here to be sound doctrine but in no way, claim my own understanding to be infallible.

It is your responsibility to weigh these things in prayer against God's word and look to Him to reveal the truths. But, be truthful with yourself and don't take license with God's word. If you come to an understanding that is in conflict with other scripture, your understanding is incorrect. God does not contradict Himself.

1 John 5:1-5 Whoever believes that Jesus is the Christ is born of God, and everyone who loves Him who begot also loves him who is begotten of Him. By this we know that we love the children of God, when we love God and keep His commandments. For this is the love of God, that we keep His commandments. And His commandments are not burdensome. For whatever is born of God overcomes the world. And this is the victory that has overcome the world—our faith. Who is he who overcomes the world, but he who believes that Jesus is the Son of God?

9 FINALLY

Before the American Industrial Revolution and the mass migration of people to the cities, a majority of the population lived a country or rural life. They depended on the Lord and their own hard work. They grew their own food and raised their own livestock. Most of the time, the entire family worked sunup to sundown with little rest. The family developed strong bonds as they toiled together to survive.

Divorce was rare because of the strong bonds formed from toiling together. Not to mention the fact that there was little time to think about it. Having an "affair" was almost impossible because there was little time and since no one really lived that close together, there was little day-to-day interaction with people outside the family.

As the American Industrial Revolution took off, many more people were living in closer proximity to each other and they had more free time on their hands. But, divorce was still frowned on and although it increased as did people having "affairs," it was not an epidemic as it is today.

As women started entering the work force and there was more interaction with those of the opposite sex at the workplace, the divorce numbers began to increase significantly. In part because there was more opportunity, but mostly because the family dynamic started to shift. Husbands and wives were spending far less time toiling together working for their survival. Instead, a large part of the day was spent at work toiling with fellow employees. In short, bonds were being built at work with fellow employees and those at home were weaker. There was far more time to entertain the idea of a different life. And more opportunity to peruse one.

Is it any wonder that now in the midst of the technology revolution, we have seen the number of divorces skyrocket? We now have websites dedicated to people looking to have an affair. Pornography is at every corner of the internet and the porn industry has exploded. A lot of today's television programming and commercials would have been considered pornographic when I was growing up.

Today's modern family is up against obstacles we could have never imagined fifty years ago. The enemy is running rampant, destroying family after family. It is now more important than ever that Christians understand the fundamentals of a strong marriage and family. That they take time to build the bonds that will hold them together.

It all centers around husbands and wives taking their correct positions in the family, fulfilling the roles God has called them to. So many times we focus on the "marriage" scriptures in Colossians and Ephesians examining them as if that is all the Bible has to say about marriage. But we must look at these scriptures in light of the whole counsel of God, under the lens of God's word. Otherwise they can become divisive. People's views on them range anywhere from seeing them as treating women as second to men, to feeling it gives men the authority to be dictators within the home.

When we examine them under the lens of God's word, as I have attempted to do here, we see that nothing could be further from the truth. There is no way these viewpoints can hold any water in light of the scriptures. In fact, Galatians 3:28 tells us there is no difference between male or female; we are all one body in Christ. It's only by studying God's word and spending time with Him in prayer that we will keep our focus where it should be. Each doing their part according to what the Lord has called them to do.

Husbands, it is imperative that you continually grow in the word, striving to be the leader you are called to be. The more you understand just how much Jesus loved the church and see the lengths that He went to, to have communion with us, the easier it will be to be the man He has called you to be. And, the easier it will be for your wife to be the woman He has called her to be.

Wives, only by being in prayer, spending time with the Lord, and studying His word, will you be able to properly submit to your husband. Jesus though equal willfully submitted to the Father, laying aside His priestly garments and became man. You have probably seen the movie *The Passion of the Christ*. They tried very hard in the movie to give you a realistic understanding of how Jesus was tortured and the physical pain He endured. But none of that came close to what He experienced when He took our sin onto Himself.

The more you understand His love for you and
see His example of submission, the easier it will
be for you to submit to your husband and the
easier it will be for him to become the man God
has called him to be.

We live in a fallen world that creeps ever closer
to the day of judgment. As we get nearer and
nearer to that day things will only get worse. But
if you trust in the Lord and follow His precepts,
your marriage will endure it. However, it's about
much more than that. If we put His precepts to
work in or marriages and our families, we will be
better equipped to also put them to work when
dealing with others. It all starts in the family. If
we can't love our husband or wife properly, how
can we ever hope to love others?

On one hand you could say it is actually easier
to forgive a stranger since you really don't spend
much time with them. You can kind of forgive
them and forget. It's not like your husband or
wife who you have constant contact with. Even
an acquaintance or a friend would be easier to
forgive than your husband or wife. At least you
don't have to live with them.

But on the other hand, if you have truly
forgiven someone, it should not matter how
much time you spend with them. I would argue

that if you are unable to forgive the trespasses of your husband or wife, then you are not truly able to truly forgive anyone. After all, this is the one you picked to spend your life with.

When we forgive we should not remember it. That means if you are in conflict with someone, past issues should not become part of the conflict. Unfortunately, many times they do and they are actually weaponized.

> *Matthew 6:18 "For if you forgive men their trespasses, your heavenly Father will also forgive you. 15 But if you do not forgive men their trespasses, neither will your Father forgive your trespasses."*

Now this is an inconvenient scripture. In Matthew 18 when Peter asked how often they should forgive their brother each day, Jesus answered with a parable about a servant that was in debt to his master. When the master demanded repayment from the servant, he pleaded with the master. The master had compassion and forgave his servant's debt completely. After leaving his master the servant immediately goes to all those that are in debt to him and demands payment. When the master finds out, guess what! He again places a demand for the wicked servant to repay his debt.

It is important that we always remember what we were saved from when dealing with others that we feel have wronged us. The debt Jesus paid for you on the cross far exceeds anything that has been done "to you." By taking all of your sin onto Himself, on the cross, He paid for all your sins and trespasses. The debt that was owed for them was death. You literally owed your life for them. What could anyone have done to you that required this type of payment? How petty it is when we refuse to forgive others that we feel have wronged us.

Isaiah 43:25 "I, even I, am He who blots out your transgressions for My own sake; And I will not remember your sins."

Some time ago I was called over to a group of young ladies that had been sitting off to the side talking. One of the girls in the group had tears in her eyes and I soon found out why. They had been talking about salvation and sin. The girl that was crying was upset because at a young age she had been raped by a couple older cousins. Since that time she had been sexually active and she seemed to be under the belief that she could not be forgiven. She could not be "pure."

What I shared with her is this. If we have accepted Jesus into our lives and repent for our sins, God will forgive them. He will remember them no more. That means that it is as if it never happened and that in God's eyes he saw her as a virgin. Think about that for a moment. If we have truly repented for our sin and have stumble again, it's the first time in God's eyes. If we go to God repenting for having "done it again," He would say, "what do you mean again?" In His eyes the previous time never happened!

Imagine if you were able to forgive your husband or wife so completely. What a difference that would make in your marriage. It's actually what we are called to do and one of the biggest battles we will have with the "inner-man." But it is a battle worth fighting. God does not expect us to be perfect, He knows the limitations we have. What He is looking for is a heart that desires perfection, that strives against the "inner-man."

The only way to win this battle is to draw near to Him. Walk in the garden with Him daily, in prayer and meditation, studying His word and keeping it close to your heart. When you fail, be quick to seek forgiveness. Do not dwell on past failures and let them keep you from moving forward. Take away the weapons of the enemy that come from guilt and shame. But, remember what you were saved from, so that you can also be quick to forgive when dealing with others, particularly your husband or wife. Remember what God has called you to do and follow His precepts regardless of what others may do.

It's a common misperception that marriage requires a lot of give and take. What it really requires is to do what God has called you to do, give and give some more, forgive and forgive some more. I'm going to steal and twist a quote from JFK. Ask not what your husband or wife can do for you, ask what you can do for your husband or wife. Obeying God's word and forgiving and blessing others even if they are not reciprocating "is" what we are called to do! Be that husband or wife God has called you to be.

Made in the USA
Columbia, SC
31 December 2018